Fifty Catericks and Pix

ISBN: 979-8-9879761-1-1

Cover and book design by Mayfly Design

Library of Congress Catalog Number: 2023915807
First Printing: 2023
Printed in the United States of America

Fifty Catericks* and Pix

(*Cat Limericks)

There Once Was

a Cat Named...

A poetic photo tale

R. W. Byhardt and M. M. Corlew

Cat Whisperers

"Time spent with cats is never wasted."

—Sigmund Freud

ACKNOWLEDGMENTS

Special kudos to our daughter, Lydia Byhardt Bollinger, LCSW, for contributing wonderful photos of her two cats, Sophie and Maeven, composing several limericks, and tastefully editing others.

Many thanks to select friends and relatives who kindly contributed photos of their feline friends in poses ranging from cute to downright embarrassing. Many of the cats depicted have/had long lives from kittenhood to senior citizens, giving ample time to record their unique and individual behavior. For those (mostly dog lovers) who believe all cats are the same, these photos and limericks suggest otherwise. While many cats share similar behavior, each has a unique personality that makes them special in a way only the humans they own can testify to.

This book stars Hobbes with co-stars Sophie, Maeven, Cosette, Ace, Millie, Dickens, Smokey, and other fabulous felines. We'd like to give their human friends the proper recognition.

Here is a listing of pet owners and their cat(s) that are featured herein.

Roger Byhardt and spouse, Marilyn Corlew, are owned by Hobbes, a male orange tabby (marmalade) and by Coco, a female longhair Torti, now waiting for them at the Rainbow Bridge.

Lydia Bollinger is ruled by Sophie, a female shorthair tricolor (white with brown and black markings), and Maeven, a female Torti.

Julie Scheife tries to control Dickens, a gray-haired tuxedo and Smokey, an all-black shorthair with penetrating green eyes. Julie and her husband own Mayfly Design who supervised the formatting and layout of this book.

Sandy Wolf is beholden to Millie, a female long haired calico kitten.

Marty Coons thinks she owns Cossette, a female tuxedo cat.

Jim Schoenfeldt is the personal slave of Ace, a male grey tabby.

Karma Denmark gets judgmental rulings from Ruth Birdie Ginsburg ("Birdie") a female Maine Coon.

Fabulous feline walk-ons are courtesy of Elmbrook Humane Society.

INTRODUCTION

Who doesn't like cute cat photos? After accumulating enough of them to require additional cloud storage on my Apple device, I decided I needed to share the wealth. But each photo required a backstory. So, after consultation with several cats of my acquaintance, they provided poetic insight into each picture. These cat consultants have given me permission to share their insights with you, but insisted the poems conform to a strict limerick formula.

Now, limericks are best known to relate rather racy tales, such as the one that starts with "There was a young lady from Exeter...." Since I expect children and sensitive adults may read this, I'll stop there and say only that the ending of that particular limerick is rather coarse. The cats made me promise to stay away from any such innuendo but stick to the rhyming sequence and meter restrictions of the limerick. That sounded simple at first, but in practice it was much like writing slightly longer haiku.

I will explain the rules they gave me. The limerick consists of five lines. Lines one, two and five must have between seven and ten syllables and all three must have the last word rhyme. Plus, all three lines must have the same number of syllables and meter, the latter being the most difficult and not always obtainable. Lines three and four must have five syllables each and also rhyme the last word. I was amazed to find how well the cats could express themselves so concisely and with such precision. On reflection, I should have surmised this given how well they express their needs with mere variations of "meow" using only intonation, volume and repetition.

I hope the reader enjoys this exploration into the deeper cat-scape and learns the lessons of life they provide.

Fifty Catericks and Pix

"MEOW THERE! I'M HOBBES.

Welcome to my little book.

Glad you're here to take a look.

Come meet the crew

Who've posed for you.

A lot of time has been took."*

* "I don't write as goodly as my humans."

Hobbes

Garfield's Twin

A twin of Garfield lives with me.

A ginger cat, quite large is he.

He looks like a pear,

All covered in hair.

Any bigger and I'd charge a fee.

Sophie & Maeven

Lydia's Two Cats

Two cats are better than one.

They can play and jump and run.

Up, down, in and out,

Twisting 'round about.

Silliest cats under the sun.

Birdie

 **RBG**

Ruth Birdie Ginsburg is her name.

She's in the feline hall of fame.

Her stance is judicial,

And not superficial,

When she's holding Court it's not tame.

Hobbes

 **Ginger Snaps**

A ginger kitty named Hobbes

Seeks some food that he then robs.

He chooses with care,

His favorite fare,

Then gulps it down in large gobs.

Chester

 ## Fat Cat

You can't give your fat to the cat.

He will not appreciate that.

He's round as a ball,

And wider than tall,

Too big for a 10-gallon hat.

Hobbes

A Tale of One Cat

I chanced to learn of a cat with one tale

Who thought it wise to stay hearty and hale,

By begging for food,

And being quite rude.

He was just being a typical male.

Sophie

Mission: Food

Sophie is a cat with a mission.

It's always for food that she's fishin'.

What food can she find?

She'll take any kind.

Eating is her only ambition.

Dickens

Krazy Kat

The way of the Kat is slightly weird.

There's no telling how his brain is geared.

Like, just to have fun,

He'll jump up and run,

As if chased by some creature he feared.

Sophie

Fourteen Pounds and What Do You Get?

She's fourteen pounds of feline vigor

That keeps getting bigger and bigger.

How much can she eat?

Hold onto your seat!

It's way more than you can figure!

Hobbes

Mousey Toy

"This ain't a mouse, but it will do.

I'll rip the hair out as I chew.

No toys in this house

Beat this fakey mouse.

I'll turn it into mousey stew."

Cossette

Post-Thanksgiving Cat

"Me-ow my, how much did I eat?

Can't get up and can't feel my feet.

Do you have a pill

To keep down the swill

I made from scarfing turkey meat?"

Smokey

Peed On

"My human wants me to read

About some cat that has peed.

Why did she do that?

Theatrical cat!

Maybe I, too, can succeed."

Hobbes

Everything Could be Food

"I creep about looking for food.

Want it fresh, not pureed or stewed.

I don't want mixed grill.

I'm sick of that swill,

I'll eat any plant to be rude."

Hobbes

 ## Not On My Clean Towels!

Towels do make a very soft bed

And will warm a cat's body and head.

Towels covered in fur

I will have to endure,

But just wait 'til he tries to get fed.

Maeven

Two-In-One Cat

"My face has a bit of plurality.

There is a line down the middle, you see.

I'm so divided,

I feel lopsided.

I must have a split personality."

Sophie

Lap Cat

I have a large cat in my lap.

She's decided to take a nap.

Now, I am stuck here

With no escape near.

I'm clearly caught in a cat trap.

Fluffy

 ## Factory Cat

"My job is to make lots of hair

And shed it about, here and there.

It takes all my time,

My hairballs sublime,

But my humans don't seem to care."

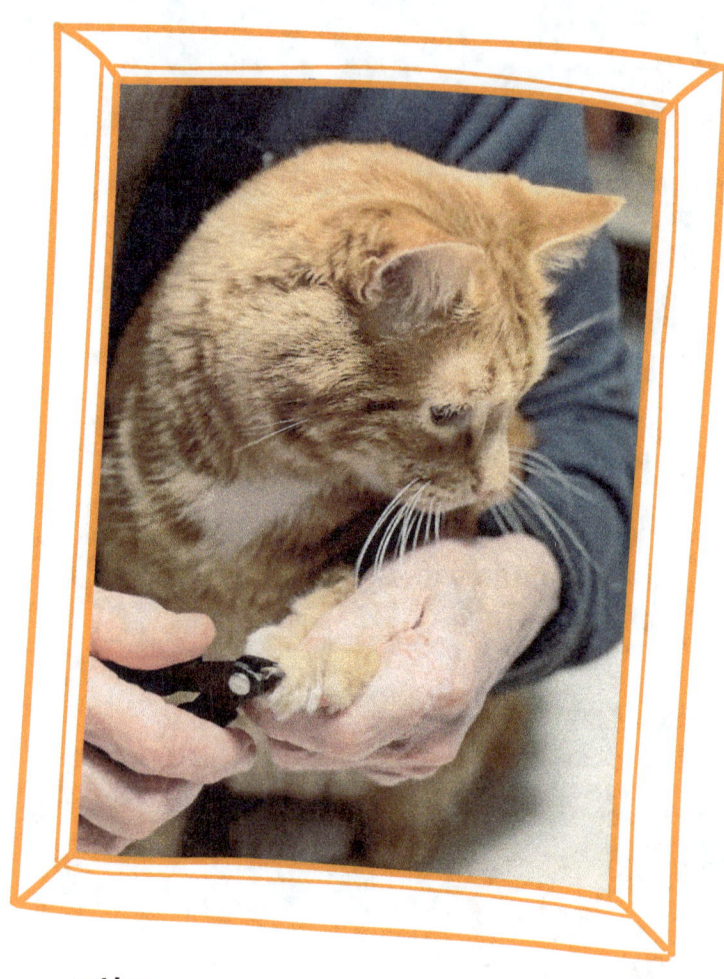

Hobbes

Nailing Things Down

At nail clip time Hobbes is a fighter.

He squirms and twists, the little blighter.

You have to go fast

Or you just won't last.

Clamp him down and hold him much tighter.

Maeven

Maeven's birthday

Maeven wanted a birthday cake.

So, she asked her humans to bake

A catnip delight,

With one candle bright.

What a celebration to make.

Hobbes

Apron Play

The cat likes to bat at apron ties.

"Come play with me" the orange kitty cries.

"The ties are a toy

For cats to enjoy.

The whole apron would be the grand prize."

Sophie

 ## Mice Beware

Fur is flying, mice are running,

Catching prey takes so much cunning.

It's no fairy tale,

This cat will prevail.

When she strikes it is quite stunning.

Hobbes

Nose Whistles

When Hobbes breathes out through
his pink nose,

While drifting off into a doze,

The air whistles out

Of his little snout.

That's better than snores, I suppose.

Sophie

Cat With A Hat

Sweet Sophie is wearing a hat.

Doctor Seuss would really like that.

A hat from a box,

And wearing no socks.

A fine outfit made for a cat.

Hobbes

 **Cat Eyes**

Yellow eyes, green eyes, or blue,

Cat's eyes are many a hue.

Looking out in slits,

Adult cats or kits,

Cat's bright eyes are watching you.

Birdie

 **Playful Birdie**

In the litter, Birdie was quite small,

She was playful and liked to maul.

She liked to eat plants

And lick up red ants.

Plus, bring home a snake or a ball.

Ace

Ace vs. the Squirrel

"That squirrel outside is a pest.

He has scared the bird from its nest.

He then eats the seed

The bird wants for feed.

He is such an unwelcome guest."

Hobbes

Kitty Cakes

Hobbes is nuts for kitty cake.

In any form they may take.

Pull out the griddle,

He's in the middle,

Begging for each one I make.

Flash

Gives Me Pause

Flash has some prodigious paws,

Armed with rather prickly claws.

He's fast as lightning,

It's somewhat frightening

When he attacks without cause.

Sophie

Puss Cat's Delight

Mai slept with her cat each night,

Much to the feline's delight.

The small ball of fur

Would meow and purr.

Both feeling safe and just right.

Hobbes

House Guard

"From my perch I guard the house.

I watch for each little mouse.

Raccoon is lurking,

And I am working

To fend off that furry louse."

Coco

Nappy

Exhausted from eating her dinner,

Leftover chicken's a big winner.

Coco in slumber,

Sawing cat lumber,

And dreaming of when she was thinner.

Ace

Ace on His Place

"I don't understand why my guy,

Bought this workout thing, why oh why?

It's perfectly fine

To call it all mine.

He does rarely give it a try."

Hobbes

I Want It Neow!

"Hey, slave, fetch me my food right neow!

That's what I mean with my loud meow.

Why are you so slow?

Just get up and go.

Open the fridge, 'cause I don't know heow."

Sophie

Puzzle Master

"My human likes puzzles of art.

And I like to tear them apart.

Here on the pieces

My pride increases,

Because this is only a start."

Cosette

I Thought I Saw A Birdee

Can Cosette catch a tropical bird?

The idea seems very absurd.

She sees it on screen.

She's the TV queen.

Cosette pounced and the picture then blurred.

Hobbes

Fruit Basket Cat

Hobbes says, "I'm gonna hatch this pear.

It's just my shape, but has no hair.

I think it will hatch,

And be a good match.

It surely will be very rare."

Leopard

 ## Cat's Lizard

At hunting the Leopard's a wizard.

He patiently stalks a small lizard.

And when he does pounce

He wastes not an ounce.

Eats it all and spits out the gizzard.

Millie

Computer Cat

All computers need a cat.

Keyboards are just made for that.

Each kitty can type

And log into Skype

So all the felines can chat.

Hobbes

High Flying Cat

Looking for our frisky cat

On a cupboard high he sat

Up by the ceiling,

Must be appealing.

Being high is where it's at.

Hobbes

 ## Cat Tunnel

A cat tunnel shaped like a shark,

Inside it is scary and dark.

To coax Hobbes to go in

There is a treat to win.

For him, it's a walk in the dark.

Sophie

Sophie's Headache

"At war I'm just a beginner

Turns out I wasn't a winner.

Mom bandaged my head

And sent me to bed.

She'll wake me in time for dinner."

Millie

Mailroom Millie

Millie likes to help with the mail.

When it comes delivered by snail.

Just letters, not bills,

Magazines with thrills

And notices telling of sales.

Hobbes

Clean Cat

Hobbes was bored with the daily routine.

He jumped into the washing machine.

A spin would be fun.

It started to run.

Big surprise! It was time to come clean!

Sophie

Sophie's House

"Welcome to my little home.

It's made of cardboard and foam.

I have swept each room

With my little broom.

It's my mini superdome."

Birdie

Singing cat

Birdie wanted humans to see

What a vocal cat she could be.

She tried hard to sing,

Attention to bring.

But was never on the right key.

Hobbes

 ## Cat Journal

"News in the Journal makes me weep.

It piles in a big bad news heap.

I don't have the need

To learn how to read.

I lie on it, then go to sleep."

Sophie

Sinking Feeling

Sophie is curled in the sink.

Why is she there do you think?

The sink's not a bed.

What thought's in her head?

Maybe she just wants a drink.

Fluffy

 **Fluffy**

Fluffy is a beautiful cat,

But she is mean for all of that.

When Dog comes around

She scratches that hound,

And has canine control down pat.

Birdie

Karma's Kat

What a cute kitten she is

Big eyes and fur all a-frizz.

But it's all I can take,

Cuz she brought me a snake.

Who knew that hunting's her biz?

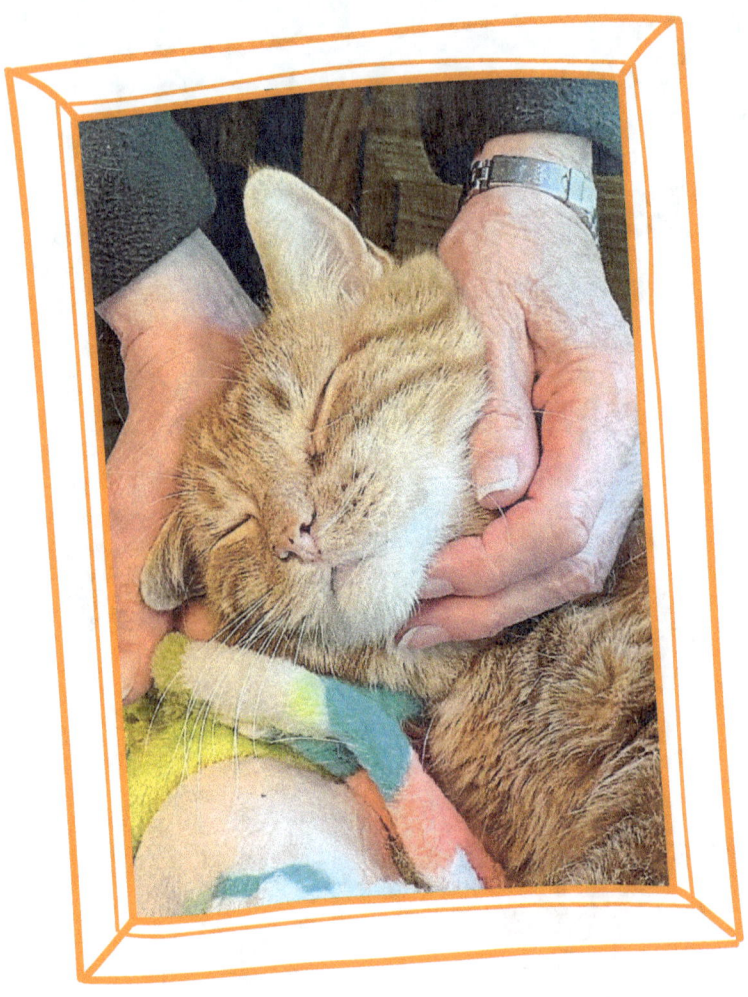

Hobbes

Warming Up the Cat

The cat likes his chin to be scratched,

Pure affection that can't be matched.

He purrs to have more

And likes to keep score

Of all the great naps he has snatched.

Hobbes

Fifty Limericks have been penned.

Thus, we have now reached THE END!

ABOUT THE AUTHORS

ROGER BYHARDT is a retired radiation oncologist who lives with his wife, Marilyn Corlew, in Brookfield, Wisconsin. They provide meal service and other duties for Hobbes—their large, always-hungry, orange tabby cat. Roger has shared his home with numerous cats in the past. Roger's limerick writing expertise was honed on limericks dedicated to graduating radiation oncology residents. These lengthy and witty poems were a highlight of the annual departmental graduation ceremonies at the Medical College of Wisconsin.

MARILYN CORLEW is a retired speech-language pathologist. Her training in linguistics and language disorders has given her a love of words and the desire to be a wordsmith. She has been converted from a dog lover to enjoying the affection of Hobbes and his predecessor, Coco, a long haired tortoiseshell cat.